Start Something, Do Something

Kelvin N. Broadus

Copyright © 2018 Kelvin N. Broadus

All rights reserved.

ISBN: 9781723864728

DEDICATION

This book is dedicated to all the hardworking employees across the nation and around the world who dream of stepping out of their cubicles and offices, and for at least one time, trying to do their own thing. Launching out into the world of entrepreneurship can be a somewhat scary thing, but just as many more have done, you can do it too.

CONTENTS

Introduction: Why There's a Need   i

1   Everyone's Not an Entrepreneur   1

2   What's Your Passion   11

3   Sponsored Hobbies   19

4   Filling a Need   30

5   Understanding Your Value   40

6   Covering the Groundwork   57

7   Tough Beginnings   71

8   Staying Motivated   81

9   Diversifying Options   93

INTRODUCTION

This book is birthed out of the common frustration that so many people feel in this society. That frustration is the problem of not having enough resources, money, to satisfy your needs and wants. And yes, if you ask anyone what they desire, you are likely to hear that they want to be rich. That is not what this is about. Rather, the aim is to focus on having enough and creating the lifestyle that you want to live according to your rules, without always being held back and told what to do by others. The idea is to find freedom and joy in what you do every day to take care of yourself, and if wealth comes along with that, even better.

In fact, the way that this book idea even came about is that one day I was sitting around trying to determine, or rather identify, one of the most aggravating things that I could imagine. After all, it is said that in your greatest frustration is the problem that you are meant to solve, and by solving this problem you will find your purpose in life. At first consideration, I thought about issues that I face (or have faced) from a personal standpoint. I considered difficulties that I have had in my personal life such as working in a location that was a two and a half hour drive from my home just to be able to cover all of my bills. I also considered being laid off due to the company that I worked for going through an acquisition and being back on the job market searching. I even considered being gainfully employed, but unhappy, and always looking for the next opportunity to take me away from it all. In either of these situations, something more is needed. Something to bring greater emotional fulfillment and financial stability is needed when such misery or financial frailty is present. Keep in mind that such a statement is not a statement of a lack of appreciation, however, especially considering that we (people in society) are so often facing tough economic times, and there are many people who don't even have jobs. Such a statement, therefore, is in no way a lack of appreciation, but rather is the recognition of the fact that if I'm constantly away from my home to be able to work so that I can pay my bills, I will never actually have the opportunity to enjoy my home, family, and the joys of such blessings. Likewise, if I have put so much of my hope into a job that then fails me, I am left in a dire situation while that company continues to move on as though I never existed. Neither of these scenarios is acceptable to me, and likely not acceptable to you for your life either. That is why as I delved deeper into this revelation, I began to think about the nature of our society as a whole and realized that this same problem that I had been facing was actually a problem that plagues the entire nation, and probably people throughout the other nations of the world as well.

There are answers to this issue though. Outside of the entrepreneurship aspect, companies that do hire can do their part. One of the most significant desires in new careers and existing jobs is being able to have more free time, especially for people who have families, and companies that go the extra mile to promote a healthy work-life balance will have an advantage over their competitors that don't. Likewise, companies that emphasize more loyalty to their employees will also have an advantage. Why is this? The reason is that we already spend the majority of our awakened hours working, so the more that can be given back to the person and their families, the better of a benefit that is provided. Even those people who don't have spouses or kids often desire more time to themselves.

Realizing this great issue, which actually is so much larger and greater than my personal situation that I originally set out to solve, is the purpose of this book though. It is not written to provide "get rich quick" advice, but is rather written to help empower others to step out and take charge of their own lives so that they can determine what type of lifestyle they deserve to live rather than having it determined by their jobs, lack thereof, or limited financial circumstances.

Start Something, Do Something

CH. 1 – EVERYONE'S NOT AN ENTREPRENEUR

It is very important that we begin this book by clarifying that everyone is not meant to be, or rather is going to be, an entrepreneur. This is so important to understand because too often people are sold on the idea of starting businesses and getting rich. There have been numerous of MLM organizations that have come and gone, making a few people rich while most of those that joined them ended up spending years wondering when and where the money would come. In fact, you really have to be careful now to make sure that you don't get drawn in to every "opportunity" to make money, work from home, and quit your job while enjoying endless vacations. This is what these businesses will declare exists for you, but in all truth, the opportunities normally are either non-existent or are only beneficial for the founders of the opportunities who will then make money off of the combined hard work done by all of the affiliates. The government officially banned Ponzi and pyramid schemes because of this, however, there are many clever companies that found loopholes to the laws and are able to market themselves as legal MLM businesses instead.

Outside of the many scams, however, one of

the main reasons that entrepreneurship isn't for everyone is that everyone cannot handle it. I will take a moment to go into more details regarding the reasons that we are so often unable to handle entrepreneurship. Please also note, that it is okay to not be an entrepreneur, and understand that the economy might not even successfully endure if everyone were entrepreneurs, completely eliminating the idea of employees (theoretically, but not proven). If you are able to find a job that you are really passionate about with a company that symbolizes the same values that you hold dear, and you'd rather have a consistent, "guaranteed" paycheck, then continuing at your current job may just be for you. There are actually many people who confidently say, "I love my job," and mean it from the bottom of their heart. If that is you, don't feel bad about it and consider yourself lucky or blessed. Considering this though, let's go into the details of the reasons that everyone cannot be an entrepreneur.

Risk Factor Tolerance

One reason that everyone cannot be an entrepreneur is because it requires a very high tolerance for risk. There's an old saying that goes, "the greater the risk, the greater the [potential] payoff." While this is true, one must make sure that he or she doesn't confuse it to think that just because there is a risk, there is a big payoff. That would be far from the truth. In fact, there are tons of so-called opportunities out there that are very risky and result in absolutely no payoff. These are what you call scams. There is another old saying that goes "every day there is a new sucker born," and unfortunately, scam artists depend in that philosophy and daily test the waters to see if they can find a "sucker" to prey upon. Scam artists come in all types of presentation, appearing like successful business owners and hustlers alike, and spend years developing their ability to influence and fool people into trusting them. In turn, we must always be vigilant in researching opportunities to ensure that they are tried and proven. We will not spend too much time discussing scam artists though, as it is better to focus on the good elements than the bad, while still being aware of all aspects of each.

The primary type of risk that comes with most entrepreneurial ventures is that of financial loss. There is <u>no guarantee</u> that any business will be successful, no matter how good the product or service is, and no matter how much certain business opportunities say that you are guaranteed to succeed. This is because success is dependent on too many factors, especially your personal effort, marketing, the current market, location, and personal commitment. Unfortunately, no one can guarantee those things. And, because you have to invest into your business, whether through a business loan, personal loans, credit cards, or bootstrapping, there is a possibility that the business will still fail and you will lose your investment. This is also why it is so important to really focus on proper preparation and planning, and to really check yourself to see if you have "tough enough skin" to handle the negative results should they appear. It is important to understand that most successful business owners have also gone through many "failures" as well, such as bankruptcies, but it was their determination and willingness to endure that allowed them to learn from those failures and overcome the obstacles before them.

Resources Available

Another challenge that many would-be entrepreneurs face is the ability or knowledge of how to obtain the necessary resources. In regards to a financial risk, it will not exist if you are never able to obtain or raise the capital to begin with. You have to have the starting funds before anything will be able to happen. Unfortunately, there are many who don't even have the confidence or drive to raise funds for themselves. Yet, one thing to understand is that if you don't have enough belief in your own idea to invest it and passionately promote it to others trying to raise the funds that you need, you cannot expect others to do so either. If you don't believe in yourself, no one else will.

"If you don't believe in yourself, no one else will."

Money isn't the only type of resource that is needed when starting a new business though. You also need good networking and marketing. If no one knows about your products or services, how can they buy them from you? Networking and marketing are often an entrepreneur's nightmare, and most creative types are very shy when it comes to self-promotion and asking for this type of support. A good business person will be willing to go to the social networking events, such as Chamber of Commerce events, to shake hands and hand out business cards to others. In this modern age, the use of social networking websites is becoming ever-more vital, just as much as how simply having a website was vital not too many few years ago. On that note, if you don't even have a website, you are really in trouble in terms of networking, so make sure that your website is on your priority list as one of the <u>foundational</u> items to have.

Finally, there are other resources such as having a strong support team and proper mentorship and/or business education. Even the wealthiest and most successful business leaders out there have mentors that they can turn to, and so should you. All of these are very important to helping your business get off the ground on a good note.

Time and Commitment

The final reason that we are going to discuss regarding why everyone cannot be an entrepreneur, though there are many more than this, is time and commitment. Starting your own business requires a LOT of time and commitment! That is something not to take lightly at all. One big reason that many small businesses fail is that the owner only has a part-time availability for what requires a full-time commitment. Business owners are known for staying at their businesses from open to close AND overtime to clean up after closing (depending on the type of business). Even online businesses often require the owner to spend endless hours coding, editing content, working out online agreements, and the like, to the point that they have very little time left to actually do the job that they enjoy, which is the very thing that they started the business for initially. When you have to spend most of your time running the administrative side of your business, you have even less time to run the actual business functions, and this can be a great challenge.

Another part that has to be considered is that people simply have lives. Many people's lives are so busy with spouses, kids, community organizations, etc., that they have very little time left over to actually work and build a business. It is true that sometimes after the business becomes more successful you'll be able to hire more people and delegate much of that responsibility that takes away so much time, but until you reach that point, you just have to do the best that you can with what you have.

Don't Be Discouraged

Please don't take the reasons why everyone is not ready, able, or capable of being an entrepreneur discourage you from going forward, if you know that this is what you need and are supposed to be doing. The warning is simply a way for you to really consider what you may be trying to get into, in order to help determine if you are making the right decision. A true proprietor actually understands and embraces these potential challenges, finding it rewarding to overcome them. If you really think about it, there is going to be some level of risk even with the traditional, "safe" job. In the traditional corporate job, there is always the risk of getting fired or laid off, finding misery due to the monotony of doing something that doesn't fulfill you, or being limited by the "glass ceiling" of wherever you are employed, whether due to imposed limitations by the leadership or just a simple lack of opportunities available. These corporate risks are, in fact, the reason that a lot of people actually decide to pursue a life of business ownership.

CH. 2 – FINDING YOUR PASSION

Now that we have a better understanding of what entrepreneurship is, it is extremely important for us to grasp the powerful sources that drives, or pushes, it. This is the difference between success and failure of any given business venture, or even any career path for that matter. This vitally important element of success is passion.

Passion, especially in terms of entrepreneurship, goes far beyond something that you really like a lot. "Really like a lot" is a phrase more appropriate for grade school boyfriends and girlfriends. Passion, on the other hand, is much more specific. Before expounding more into the nature of passion, however, let's first consider an example of how important passion is to maintain the type of persistence and commitment needed to continue towards a truly successful effort.

Example: Job

Can you imagine getting a brand, new job after being without work for an extended period of time? For many people, the excitement of getting a new job would place them into a mental state close to a child on Christmas day. The person's eyes are wide open in anticipation. Actually, most of the time, they were already in a state of awe before ever getting the job, often saying things like, "I don't care WHAT the job is in, I just really NEED one and will do WHATEVER IT TAKES to be the best I can be in it when I get one." Yes, there is something special about getting a new job.

Then, when the employee starts the new job, he/she works with intensity, fervency, and a genuine respect and appreciation for the company and tasks that he/she has been so entrusted with. Month after month, the employee is pushing out the great numbers, until...

About a year has passed and now everything is starting to seem commonplace. The job now seems more like a chore than the great gift that it once was and the employee that was once thankful for this great opportunity is complaining about the tedious tasks, insufficient pay, and lack of fulfillment.

Explanation

There is an explanation for the drastic change in the example above. The example simply demonstrates the difference of excitement and passion. Simple excitement of a new job, or business, is similar to infatuation in a relationship, whereas passion is more comparable to true love. In the prior example, the employee was excited over a new opportunity, but not passionate about it. This is why the energy faded so quickly. Don't get me wrong, passions can change, especially in business, but usually passions only change after they have been fulfilled; NOT because of challenges!

One of the best ways to determine what your passion is, is to think about yourself and what you like to do more than anything. Your passion is something that you would do for free each and every day if needed. Even better, it is something you would desire to do every day, even for free, and so the idea of getting paid for it will typically make you feel guilty for receiving pay for it (because you see it as something that you would just do regardless), or any payment is just considered "icing on the cake."

Another way to help explain your passion is that it is something that truly drives or moves you. When you are in the element of your passion, you are at your happiest and most peaceful. There is something that is even rejuvenating about it. That's why, when someone says that it drives you, this can literally be meant as though your activity in doing it seems to be on "auto-pilot," as you can do this hobby, task, etc., without even having to really think about it. Some people will try and say that their passion is making money, but that is a bit of a cop-out. Making money may be the result of your passion, but it is too vague and is much more of an outcome than an initiating, driving force. The passion is more related to the "how" you are going to grow financially and less about the end. You can also help determine your passion by listening to what other people have to say about you as well.

Many times, friends and family can help you to identify your passion because they see you from a more objective standpoint. That is, they can see the big picture, whereas you can only see it from a more subjective perspective. You can often be so close to what you are doing each and every day that you fail to see what is beyond you. Consider the young kid who wants to be a famous singer. He is so tunnel-vision about his dream that he no longer sees the value in going to school and graduating high school because he believes that he is going to be so successful that he will not need it anyway. This kid believes that he doesn't want to have to listen to what other people tell him to do, and that quitting school and having his own successful music career will solve everything. Because of this tunnel-vision, however, he is about to make a terrible mistake that will actually sabotage him in the long run, because he doesn't see how even those classes that he doesn't want to take are instilling valuable lessons on patience, endurance, commitment, wherewithal, and discipline. He doesn't understand that if he doesn't even have enough self-discipline to go through high school classes, then he likely will not have enough to push HIMSELF through the challenges that come with business ownership (beyond the fun part of doing your passion). After all, if the only thing that we needed to be successful was passion, then everyone could do it, but we need so much more. We do need that industry and business knowledge. We do need to understand financials, taxes, and legal situations, or at least have trusted advisors that do know this information. And regarding the whole concept of an objective view, we need help seeing beyond our own subjective view because often there are levels to our talent that go far beyond what we see and we actually will LIMIT ourselves from our potential because we won't step outside of our comfort zone of talent. That young musician in the example could be so stuck in the idea of singing R&B that he never realized how much better he could do as a Country singer, and by simply having access to some others outside of himself, like family members, they can explain to him how much more he has to offer.

Understand that this is not saying that anyone should really be pursuing something outside of his or her passion, but rather that we should allow ourselves to remain open to that which lies BEYOND our passion. Another way of putting it is that we have to be willing to push our passion to a whole, new level. In scriptures, we read that our gift will make room for us. One way to interpret this is that our talent will open doors. We just have to be willing to recognize those doors and allow the passion within us that is related to those doors to push us into succeeding beyond our comfort zones.

CH. 3 – SPONSORED HOBBIES

It is very important that we discussed discovering and following your passion in the previous chapter, because sometimes it can be that very passion that can pave the way for your success.

This success is not necessarily in terms of a traditional job, but in terms of sponsorship. And, when you look across the spectrum of the business world, sponsorship is definitely at play in everything from professional athletics to YouTube stars and beyond. That is, sponsorship is definitely not a new thing in business by any means. It is something that has been around for quite some time. The truth is that some of the greatest wealth in the world is found through sponsorship/advertising, as this is the very practices that fuels television stations and mass media.

Since I've brought this up, let us consider for a minute just how television and radio stations operate. Have you ever wondered where the TV networks get their funds from to be able to pay the high salaries of the actors, and where radio stations get the money to pay the DJs, artist royalties, and the many promotions and concerts? Television networks get virtually all of their money from advertising. The philosophy behind it is that, if a show is created that is so entertaining, awesome, etc., that millions of viewers are willing to watch it consistently week after week, then those millions of viewers are also potential customers of various companies. The advertising companies, then, are willing to pay millions of dollars' worth of advertising so that their products or services can be seen by all of these viewers, potentially enticing the viewers to go out and buy that product or service. This is why the networks have to work so hard to remain relevant and exciting while also being considerate of the standards of the said advertisers. Without the advertisers, the networks would be broke and eventually go out of business. In a sense, the advertisers are "sponsoring" the media that is produced by the television networks so that they can reach the viewers of that content.

Likewise, the same is considered with radio. If the radio station is playing "good music" that is drawing a lot of listenership, companies are more than willing to shell out large amounts of money to make sure that all of those interested listeners are able to hear about their great product or service.

Businesses will engage in sponsoring activities such as special giveaways in order to entice more interaction, all while using it to get their name "out there" to the general public. I also mentioned all of the special contests, concerts, and promotions, however, so that you will be able to get an idea of just how much money is being made. These stations are making enough money to not only pay the many salaries of the employees, from DJs to sound engineers, to producers, in addition to being able to sponsor major artist concerts, cruises, and more. If you have listened to any major radio station lately, you too have heard these, often promoted by having listeners to call in by a certain time and the station will accept a certain numerically identified caller, usually based on the station's frequency identification. Pay attention to the contest, as they will say something such as, "brought to you by…," as they are announcing the prize being offered. These are some of the most prominent and classic forms, but there are many more, and newer ways that sponsorship occurs on the individual level. At the individual level, you and I all have the ability to also get paid by sponsors as an alternative income to the traditional methods.

Because sponsorship doesn't stop there, YOU are provided with a great opportunity to change YOUR life around using the very thing that you enjoy and are passionate about, if you're willing to work on it. Have you ever watched a NASCAR race, Extreme Games, UFC, or any other major sporting event? If so, you'll notice that the individuals (cars for car sports), the field/track/ring/etc. that the sport is being played on, and the commercials being aired during the event are all sponsors. If it were not for the sponsors whose logos are plastered all over those NASCAR cars, the racing teams would not have the funds to compete. These sponsoring companies are carrying the majority load of the costs associated with participating in the sport. They are helping to pay for the cost of the cars, the salary of the drivers, the maintenance crew, and the operating expenses, just to get their business names seen by the hundreds of thousands of viewers that tune in and attend the different events. And I know that you might say, "well those are big sports and I don't have the skills to play/do those, so that is out of the question for me." Yet, it doesn't have to be the most popular thing YET in order for you to do it.

In fairness, the Extreme Games are fairly new in comparison to the more traditional sports, but they have managed to garner so much attention that the sponsors have rushed right to them. Some prominent energy drink companies have really began to provide a lot of sponsorship to many of the extreme sports events in the past decade or so. Likewise, even more nowadays, games like yo-yos and cup stacking have become popular enough to gain sponsorship, creating FULL-TIME, and FULL SALARY positions for the people that compete in them. Who would've imagined!?!

It's not completely the sport or game that brings the sponsorship though, it's the excellence that it is done with. The reason that people have been able to gain sponsorship for these things is because they have mastered the games or sports so well that it draws attention from masses of people, and advertising is all about gaining massive attention from potential clients and customers. What I am telling you is that if you find ANYTHING that YOU can do exceedingly well, as in better than most to the point that you virtually make an "art form" out of it, you can be successful at it making a good salary through sponsorship. This can be through a game, a sport, a special talent or gift… it doesn't matter as long as it is something that you do well enough to draw tons of attention. This is what created the great online video social site boom, where people were becoming rich and famous virtually overnight over one or two videos that became extremely popular, as in millions of views. This continues to happen over and over again, and will probably not be ceasing any time soon.

Not too long ago, there was a video (that most

of you would probably remember) of a young man who responded to a news reporter about a break in by a rapist. This young man purposefully was very "elaborate" and entertaining in order to bring more attention to the terrible situation, telling viewers to hide their wives, kids, and husbands. The moment that the news report went online, he became an instant internet sensation, and now even makes income from that video clip. People have made music to it, and created all types of media that are making money, all from this one video clip. This man has even managed to get roles in movies and TV appearances from this original moment of fame, allowing him to break free from the standard 9-5 grind and live is life according to his own terms.

It doesn't have to be based around video, music, or anything in entertainment at all though; it does have to be based around skill, PASSION, and talent. These keys are the keys that unlock the doors to followers, and followers unlock the doors to advertising, as the more fans, followers, supporters, etc. that you have, the more that advertisers will want to jump on the bandwagon to put their "faces" out there to be seen. There have been people on YouTube who have made careers from sponsorship of their hair styling or make-up tutorial videos. There have also been people who have gained sponsorship for gross things like pimple popping videos. There is a young kid who gained a great income by reviewing toys on YouTube, and he hasn't even gotten out of elementary school. The list of YouTube stars goes on and own.

Beyond YouTube, there are many other social media apps, with newer apps being created on a regular basis. With each new social media fad, even more success stories occur. Instagram is full of people who have launched "modeling" careers by posting hundreds of selfies and photos from their everyday lives. Some users of Instagram have actually done so well with gaining followers of their image content, that they charge people high fees for shout outs and promotions on their popular pages. The more they are seen, the more money they make, so this symbiotic relationship remains as an "all-time great" in terms of making income.

An important lesson in all of the sponsorship opportunities and successes is that there is a certain psychology to it all and that if you can demonstrate something that is so appealing that it inspires others, creates desire from others, or allows others to live vicariously through you, then you have something on your hands by which you can get paid through sponsorship. That concept is definitely worth repeating.

"Demonstrate something that is so appealing that it inspires others, creates desire from others, or allows others to live vicariously through you."

The Instagram models that are making a living from their posts are using their sex appeal, beauty, and charisma in order to draw huge crowds of people to their pages, and then flipping those views into opportunity. It is successful for them because their fans either want to be just like them or want to be with them. The athlete is so powerful and effective that his or her fans wish that they were as powerful, agile, or skilled, and dream about being the same way. Even the entertainer who is demonstrating a talent such as singing, dancing, or acting is able to inspire other aspiring artists and entertainers to do more because they visualize themselves with that same powerful voice, grace, or stage presence. Inspire enough people and there will automatically be a place for you to gain income from it.

CH. 4 – FILLING A NEED

One area of entrepreneurship that is never maximized is the area of fixing problems. Many people like to pursue dreams that are very personal to them, as in ego related businesses that self-serve instead of serving the masses. Yet, there is a great opportunity in making it about others and solving other people's problems, because other people are going to be the ones that are supporting you as your customers. Think about this. As long as we are in an imperfect world, there will always be things that need to be done, fixed, changed, corrected, etc., and because of this, there will always be opportunities for would-be entrepreneurs to start new businesses. I'll even go a little further as to say that as long as there are rich people with big egos and/or arrogant idealism, there is always room for new businesses to be developed. These new businesses are created and developed because a need is being filled, whether it is creating a solution or just making someone feel better about themselves than they already feel.

Regardless though, as long as there are needs that have to be filled, and problems that have to be solved, there are businesses to be started. Let's look at some examples of products that made people millionaires simply by solving problems and filling needs.

Examples

- Social Media – One of the best examples, in one of the largest and most influential areas, is social media. Think about how it originally started. Social media was not created to become as large as Facebook, gaining governmental influence around the globe. It was simply about building website platforms to keep people with similarities (such as people going to the same colleges, or musical artists) connected on the web. It was something that was created to help people socialize and increase their network with like-minded people, which beforehand was somewhat difficult, especially for introverts. By solving this problem, social media has now become a staple of modern culture that people from all walks of life cannot live without… a huge success.

- Mobile Phones – It goes without saying that social media, and many more apps and services online, would not be as successful without smartphones. Let's go back even further though, to the original mobile phones that didn't even have internet access. Originally, they were created to solve the problem of communication on the go. People had to find pay phones (in sometimes, dangerous areas) and hopefully have enough money in their pockets, in order to communicate while away from home or work. It was survivable, but it also was pretty inconvenient. There were stages that led up to the smaller, individual phones, such as the large car phones, but eventually the creation of a smaller, personalized device made everyone's lives easier.

- Paper Clips – While this is a very classic example, it is important to know what it is so valid. Paper clips are very simple tools consisting of a single piece of wire bent in a certain manner. There is no major technology in them, yet even in this high-tech world, they are very important in utilized heavily in the business and educational world. When you consider how you see them at literally every office that you go to, then you can understand how these relatively cheap tools still generate a very large amount of money. The lesson in analyzing the success of these simple tools like paper clips, or even sticky notes, is that it doesn't have to be some huge, elaborate creation in order to be successful. Sometimes, it can just be practical.

Speaking of things being practical, that is one of the best attributes of starting new businesses for the new entrepreneur. As a new entrepreneur, you will likely not have a large amount of capital or resources to do great and elaborate things. You will also not likely have the technology to develop major website backed businesses online. What you will have, however is ambition, drive, and whatever resources are currently in your hand. Some of the most common ventures to start are based on the practical needs that we personally experience. In other words, a person may be sitting around and thinking, "I wish that I had someone who could do…." In the realization that there is currently no such service, a new business is then born. Sometimes, the best way that the need is discovered is from a standard frustration that a person is facing, and so they work diligently to resolve the issue for themselves. Once they solve this issue for themselves, it only makes sense to them that there are probably MULTITUDES of others out there who are facing the same issue, and by solving that problem (or filling that need), the entrepreneur finds success in his/her goals. Some of the most successful entrepreneurs I know have done extremely practical ventures such as daycare centers, driving schools, resume writing services, or cleaning services. It is in such practical need, that there is almost always opportunity. It is also in such practical areas that you can expect to maintain a decent income. Therefore, if you just want to start something, and don't really have any direction – you just want to create anything to make more money – consider things that are practical as your first and easiest options.

Caution on Procrastination

As a word of caution when considering any need that you are trying to fill, please know that you are not the only person in the world experiencing that need or issue. If you were, there would be no market existing for you to be able to be successful with it. In fact, as mentioned before, there are multitudes of people who are also experiencing the same issue, which is why the market exists in the first place. Because of this, you must not delay in stepping out and building your product, service, or brand!

Many people have learned the hard way how procrastination affects success. Think of all of the times that you, yourself, have had a great idea about a product or service and thought that you should do something about it, and then sat on that idea. Then, think about how you felt when that exact same product that you were THINKING ABOUT creating, actually appears on the shelves of your local store or on some television infomercial. It is not a good feeling at all. Yet, so many people face this issue all the time because of a failure to act on it. I actually have people close to me who have been very disappointed that they didn't act on the idea that they were previously considering. Everything from the "stay cool" pillow to the air ionizer were discussed in my presence before someone else ended up actually creating it. If there is a need to be filled and no one has done it yet, then you better believe that someone else, sooner or later, is going to do it, so it might as well be you. And, just because someone else does it before you do doesn't mean that anyone stole your idea. Other people are just as smart and are capable of solving problems and filling needs as well. It is a competitive market, so you might as well get in the game and make some power plays!

Improving Existing Products

In addition to filling needs by creating new products or services, sometimes the need is there because of a failure in existing products or services. Maybe, you are looking for a good chiropractor because there are none in your area (or those in your area provide terrible work), and so you decide to go to school to learn the practice for yourself and do it the right way where you live. Maybe you are going to become a barber because you cannot find a qualified barber who knows how to cut your type of hair, so you finish school and start your own shop. Maybe you don't like the way you are treated in the local nail salon and so you take on the trade of esthetician and open your own shop to cater to you and your friends, plus any others that would come as the word of your excellent service spreads.

Another way of looking at it is in the improvement of some existing products. Sometimes the need is created because the existing products in the market are of low quality. For example, the concept of the cooling pillow is the improvement on an existing product. If you look at the smoking industry, you can see how different smoking devices have been created and improved upon over the years. Even when you look at things as simple as construction tools, there are improvements on things like hammers and wrenches. Many of you reading this book can understand a situation where you may have been using a particular product and said to yourself, "I wish that there was a better…" In this situation, the entrepreneur's mind will often automatically default to the idea of improvement. Products, services, and ideas alike can always be improved upon. And you don't have to worry about whether the idea or product is patented, because even though you cannot take something that is patented, improvements or variations to that which is existing is allowed. Note: It is advisable for you to consult an attorney for all of the ins and outs for any ideas that you are thinking of creating. Nevertheless, this is all about the conceptualization, but it is also very important to spend some time discussing your psychological standpoint.

CH. 5 – UNDERSTANDING YOUR VALUE

At this point in your entrepreneurial journey, you will have thought about the amazing and fantastic idea for your new business or venture, and you are excited. You have taken those initial steps to set up your business (which we will go into in more detail later), and are ready to put it out there for the world. Or, maybe you have come up with the business plan and are looking for investors or setting up your prices. In the area of setting up your prices, this is where a lot of business people sell themselves short. Don't get me wrong, a lot of people sell themselves short in life in general. Think about how many people have been in relationships with people who were truly not worthy of them, or at jobs that didn't pay them what they were worth. In fact, one of the top reasons that so many people are actually seeking their own ventures is because they are at a point where they feel like they are not being properly rewarded for the value that they are bringing to the table. Whenever you are giving your all towards something or someone and it seems like they are not giving you your worth in return, also known as taking you for granted, it creates a sense of resentment that is difficult to move past. When it comes to business related issues, it can be so discouraging that you may even start to lose your initial motivation and decide to give up on your dreams altogether. This is not what we want for any of you, and that is why it is so important to really start figuring out what your services are worth and properly pricing it based on your value and the value of what you are offering. There are a few things to consider along the way, including market value, desired salary, and supply and demand. We will briefly discuss all three of these.

Market Value

The first thing to consider when establishing your prices, or the value of your worth in the marketplace is industry standards. By all means, you will, or should, always determine that you are worth the highest value in the world as a matter of self-confidence and self-worth. In the marketplace, however, despite how good you feel about your work, it doesn't mean that the rest of the world will feel the same way. This is why we do comparisons in order to establish what people are really willing to pay for and why they are willing to pay that price for it. Consider how many "wannabe" music artists are out there and THINK that their music is amazing, but yet the market would think if it as garbage. We, as entrepreneurs, don't ever want to be in a situation where people are looking at our product or service as garbage while we are marketing it everywhere is as some spectacular thing of which we are charging an arm and a leg. So how do we establish market prices?

Most businesses or services that we would begin already have been started somewhere by others before us. Because of that, we typically have a good starting point in our venture. Even if there is no existing business quite like ours, we can still find something that is similar enough to ours to base our pricing from. When we are looking at any existing business, however, we must also consider the clout of that business. How long has this business been around? What are their credentials? What is their customer base (local individuals, businesses, large corporations, etc.)? How much money are they pulling in per year?

Questions like these help us tremendously because they help us gain a realistic point of view regarding how we should set our prices. For example, I began a personal training/fitness coaching business (Kilo Bravo Fitness). To establish prices in comparison to the market, I began to research other personal trainers, and looked at their hourly prices. Among those that I found prices for were trainers who have been in the industry for YEARS. Some of these trainers have competed in, and won, national and international bodybuilding competitions. They also have developed their own bodies and routines to that which is much more advanced than my own. Knowing this, should I price my services (as a brand new personal trainer who hadn't been certified even a full year) the same as them? Typically, no. My experience and qualifications don't compare, and knowing that, it would be wiser for me to price my services slightly lower. After all, I have to look at it as if I were the client and how I would compare the different options that are there. If I were shopping around for a new personal trainer and I saw a trainer with 8 years of experience, competition experience, and a degree in exercise science advertising for the same hourly rate as a new trainer with less than a year of experience, no competition, and a degree in communication… I would go for the first trainer at the same price. That is a "no brainer." On the other hand, if the new trainer, who is demonstrating some real skill in his personal transformation and who has great interpersonal skills is selling me in a price that is 25% less per hour with a trial class to check out his service for free, I would likely at least give it a try and see what happens from there.

That is the type of thing that we have to consider as entrepreneurs, how the customer thinks. Our competition in the marketplace does give us great insight into that though. Whatever business or service that you are starting, make sure that you take the time to really canvass your regional area for existing prices and truly understand why they are setting their prices in that manner. Without affording yourself this necessary due diligence, you stand to bring embarrassment and discrediting to yourself, your brand, and your name. A person who doesn't know how to reasonably set the standards of price for their own business is not equipped to be massively successful. Don't get me wrong, even if you manage to get a few clients, customers are discerning enough to know when they are being ripped off by being charged more than the value of the product or service.

Desired Salary

Another element for the new business owner to consider is what their desired salary would be if this were their full time job. In essence, it is their job or career. Business ownership is similar to a job except that you are paying yourself for the work that you are doing instead of someone else paying you. Likewise, you are responsible for being your own manager (time management, work ethic, completing your tasks), and your own CEO (setting the vision and strategic moves for your business). With this being considered, you determine what you would deserve or like to be paid annually for that type of work. Please note, however, that you should set your desired salary for a higher rate than if you were just an employee because you are responsible for your own management and vision leadership. Therefore, ideally, you would want to determine a salary for yourself that would be equivalent of the higher rate from your upper management levels if you were at a corporation.

With that in mind, you have a simple calculation to determine the hourly rate for what you are doing. Take the desired annual salary from your business and divide it by the 52 weeks in the year, then divide that by the 40 hours of a standard work week. This will give you your hourly rate for the work you are doing. At this point, you determine your standard hourly rate. In the example below, I will show the rate for myself as a personal trainer if my goal is to make $100,000 per year.

$100,000 ÷ 52 weeks = $1,923.08/week
$1,923.08 ÷ 40 hours = $48.07/hour

Based on the above calculation, my hourly rate would be $48/hour (in the most simplified analysis). In that example, I would ideally charge my clients $48/hour, however, in comparison of how close those with much more experience have, I might lower it to $40 or $35 per hour starting out (depending on my local market comparisons). And, of course, if I am going to stick to my $48/hour, then I had better make sure that in the comprehensive nature of my services, that I am truly earning that rate.

This was a simpler rate calculation, however. In other industries, such as coaching or public speaking (as I am also a public speaker), you cannot look at it from the point of how long your speech lasts. For instance, if I wanted to make that same salary as a public speaker, I would not charge $48/hour for the speaking engagement. That would be extremely foolish. Instead, I have to consider the amount of time that I put into developing the speech/presentation and all of the additional costs to put it together. This is where pricing gets a little more complicated. Say for instance, I spent two weeks putting together my training session for a client. That two weeks includes my research, development of the presentation that I am using, my quality checks, and my rehearsing and polishing up of the training. My calculated rate above was already $1,923/week. We'd round that up to $2,000 times the two weeks, so we're now at $4,000 for the training session. Then for the actual training classroom time, we're still adding the $48, let's say $50/hour, for each hour of classroom time. Finally, we'd add additional fees or approximately $500-$1,000 for administrative fees to cover your personal management costs, plus any costs for supplies like giveaways and client-specific decorations that you would use during the training session. At this point, the training session (depending on how long the classroom time lasts) could easily be between $6,000 and $8,000. Even with that standard, however, you would then compare your estimate to that of your competition to ensure that you are offering the best deal to secure the business of your customer, without sacrificing too much of your worth (the annual salary that you determined). This form of salary determination is a standard practice, but it's not all-inclusive, which is why we also use the additional elements of the comparison of the market price and supply and demand.

Supply and Demand

Supply and demand are concepts that you will find in any standard college business class. In a simplified explanation, you can describe it by saying that the greater supply of a product that is available to the public, the lower the demand. Likewise, when you limit the supply of a desired product, the public will demand it more and therefore you can raise the price. Of course, the concept is much more in-depth and many of the readers of this book will be familiar with the principle.

Regarding this principle, we have to then reflect upon how it relates to us as entrepreneurs. Every product that we have created or every service that we offer does NOT have a high demand in our targeted marketplace. For some businesses, there is always a need, but even those can become saturated markets. For example, if you look at how many attorneys are in any city, even a small city, there are hundreds or more. Attorneys is always a saturated market, and this is why the keywords for attorneys are always so expensive in search engine marketing. Because it is such a saturated field, you have to be that much more competitive with your pricing and with your marketing. The good thing is that it is a field that demands and retains the higher hourly rate based on the mere nature of the business. Every field, product, or service isn't as "lucky" though.

You may really be passionate about your coin collecting business and your supply is low, but that doesn't mean that you can place a high price on your services or products because the demand might just not be there, despite the scarcity of it. On another note, your new night club, in a city with many night clubs, might still have a high demand because of its unique qualities and still justify higher entrance fees and VIP service rates. Supply and demand help to guide us in the adjustment of the rates that we have established by the other methods mentioned before. For example, if you have established a solid fee based on the market value for your qualifications and your desired salary, but realize that there is a low demand because of the high supply of other competitors, this might lead you to run some introductory specials such as free or reduced-price (even half-priced) services for a short amount of time. In a saturated market, this can help you to stand out amongst your competitors for long enough to convert them into full-fledged clients. This is what you want, clients that are paying full price as close to your established rate as possible.

Even beyond those clients that are paying you at your established rate, you must continue working at your craft and improving it constantly. You must continue to strive to be the best in your industry and fight for that title. In doing so, you begin to separate yourself from the rest of the crowd, which makes your product or service less common. After all, any good product or service is going to be duplicated somewhere or at some point. By perfecting yours and constantly improving it, that will automatically cause YOUR supply to be reduced while your demand to be increased. As this occurs, you will start becoming more justified in raising your rates higher than your originally established rates. What you have becomes so appealing that you have to reduce its accessibility. If you think about it, this will make sense, but I will provide you with some examples to further explain and drive the point.

Music producer, and mogul, Timbaland, had to earn his stripes just like any other producer. He spent years as a music producer, with some of the acts who later also became famous, such as Missy Elliot, Aaliyah, and Ginuwine. He even spent some time working under the guidance of Devante Swing before he became extremely well-known. As the years went by, and he kept developing his craft, he gained more notoriety and fame. Then, at the top of his game, Timbaland ended up becoming one of the highest paid music producers in the industry. In fact, his music became so highly coveted that man artists actually began to brag on the fact of being able to afford one of his beats. Just the same, you can also keep improving your product or service to the level that the demand drastically increases. Because of the high demand increasing so much that you literally cannot service all of the people who want you, the supply is automatically lowered.

Another example that we can use is my other industry, personal training. When you do one-on-one personal training, it can require a lot of personal TIME. Each session lasts about an hour, and there are only so many working hours in a day, at least that you want to spend working. Because of this, there is an automatic limit on supply. Sure, when you are just starting out, you are seeking as many clients as possible and often doing the same even after you have become established. But, imagine for a moment that you become hugely successful and highly recognized. Let's say that you book a client who happens to be a huge celebrity. At that point, your name is going to be "out there" and people will start lining up at your door to seek YOUR services. Your demand, because of the fame and recognition, become so great that you cannot fit all of those customers in a reasonable day. At this point, you will have to create waiting lists, and more exclusive requirements for one-on-one personal training. As a side note, can then branch out to your online training options and pre-packaged workout plans to help ease the demand, but even then, you still will be able to require a much higher rate for your personal and customized online training than ever before. At that point, you can truly know that your business has been a great success (not to take away from all of the preceding successes).

Value Summary

In all of these methods to establishing value, and knowing your worth, it is important to still recognize that you, and only you, can ultimately determine your worth. There are some experts in who can easily demand five digits for a keynote speech (and get paid that amount), yet will occasionally provide one for a fraction of that for the purpose of a certain audience, or to give back. There are some consultants and coaches that can require hundreds of dollars per hour (and also get paid that amount) for their coaching sessions – as in, webinars – and yet they occasionally offer specials as low as $10 for webinar signups. In the world of elite bodybuilding, a legend such as Kai Greene has occasionally offered his training eBooks for as low as $10, and he could charge far more than that at his level. These types of decisions are more related to marketing than self-worth as their worth has been solidly established in their industries.

Whatever the situation though, it is important that you take the time to do the research, give yourself HONEST evaluation of the product or service that you are offering, and weigh all of these components to determine what is the proper valuation of yours. Once you do this, you can more forward to some of the other elements to entrepreneurship related to the legalities and accounting. Ultimately though, make sure that you don't sell yourself short in the process as you establish your worth. Establish what you deserve, but also earn what you are demanding.

CH. 6 – COVERING THE GROUNDWORK

DISCLAIMER: The information found within this chapter (or the book overall) does not constitute professional legal or accounting advice, and is solely the opinion of the author, based on personal experience and methods. Techniques and suggestions described are simply information, and what works for some may not work for others. There is no guarantee of anyone's success or failure as it depends on each individual's personal effort and thoroughness. It is recommended that you consult with a practicing attorney for all legal advice as well as a Certified Public Accountant for all financial and taxation guidance, as well as any specific governmental entities that apply.

When it comes to covering the initial groundwork of whatever business that you are stepping out and starting, there are quite a few things to consider. These considerations include the right business model for your work, long-term or end goal planning, as well marketing, so a well thought out plan is very important and quite essential for any entrepreneur that intends on being successful in his or her business efforts. We will discuss aspects of these different components to provide some ideas for you to contemplate as you begin setting the foundation of your business. We will discuss different business models and the levels of establishment, as well as marketing types throughout the chapter.

Business Structure

The first thing that we will look at are the different types of business structures. Ideally, in any business, you will need to determine whether you want your business to be a Sole Proprietor, a Partnership, a Limited Liability Company (LLC), a Corporation, or a Non-Profit Organization. Each of those formats has its own benefit or use. Note: You can also get a lot of information on these different structures from the Internal Revenue Service (IRS), including details found on their website, www.irs.gov, as well as from your state's Secretary of State office. The IRS provides you with your Tax ID number (also known as an EIN), while you incorporate (if applicable) through your Secretary of State. Your Tax ID number is something that you will obtain no matter what business structure that you establish, as it is the federal government's way of tracking the income and taxes for your business. Even non-profit organizations will obtain these, despite some entities not being required to pay taxes. Beyond that, you would go to your local government for a business license, to ensure that all of the relevant parties are covered in the process.

With the option of Sole-Proprietorship, you as a business owner are simply identifying that you, individually, are fully responsible for this business. What that means is that all liability for the business falls on you. If someone wants to sue the business, they are actually suing you as the individual and you take the full responsibility for everything in that situation. Likewise, when you file taxes, you are filing those taxes with your personal taxes each year. With all of the potential liabilities that come with it, there are also some benefits to it as well. For one, it is the easiest to establish and doesn't require an additional incorporation. This means that you don't have to pay the incorporation fees, which also makes it less expensive to begin. For a small business that is just starting out, this can make a huge difference as many don't have the initial start-up capital needed to establish themselves in the other structures. Another benefit is that the owner is able to get started faster because of the lesser paperwork that needs to be filed. Many individuals who are trying to "hit the ground running" will find this extra efficiency helpful, because there is no delay in getting started; they can typically be up and running within a day or two, as you can receive your EIN in the same day that you apply for it. A final benefit of being a sole-proprietor is that it is an individual structure. You don't have to get other people involved in the process, but rather are able to go forward as you deem necessary. This is helpful because in other structures, you need other people to be indicated in the paperwork to establish them.

A second business structure that is available is the Partnership structure. The partnership is very similar to the sole-proprietorship, except that it is done by multiple people. In other words, you handle things on your taxes like an individual, but the business belongs to multiple people. For instance, two attorneys can create a practice together and both mutually share the liabilities and profits. The business doesn't stand as its own entity, but it is rather like two or more sole-proprietors that are working together on the same efforts. If you have some business partners that you really trust, who are on the same level of commitment, and who you are confident that they will not sabotage you in the future, then this may be a good option. It will give you the option of pooling your resources together and sharing the burdens of business ownership with each other, which can be very helpful. The danger is that it is often not the wisest to mix business and friendship together, as often one, or both, will end up coming to its demise. Obviously, this isn't always the case, however it is something to be aware of when establishing your structure. Beyond these two, we have those which take away more liability, the LLC and the Corporation, which we'll also discuss in more detail.

The Limited Liability Company, aforementioned as the LLC, is one of the most popular business structures that is used by entrepreneurs. One of the reasons are found in the name itself. This structure provides a sense of protection to the business owner, limiting their liability from negative things such as financial loss and lawsuits. With an LLC, the business will be seen legally as its own entity. That is, it is treated like a person for general taxation purposes. This structure requires a little more in terms of paperwork, such as filing it with the Secretary of State and when you complete the paperwork, you must also have "officers" indicated, which can include yourself. For instance, when I set up a previous LLC, I was required to have three officers. For many new entrepreneurs, the officers chosen are usually CEO (the business owner), CFO, and Secretary, or some similar combination. A lot of new business owners will also use members of their household as the other officers. As the owner of the LLC, you typically make the decisions of the business, but it is helpful to have officers that you can trust for input. Also, for taxation, the LLC can typically file its own taxes, but sometimes the owners will file the taxes for the business with their own personal taxes. Your attorney and accountant can help you tremendously in this area. One of the other great benefits in this structure is that even though it is treated as its own entity, the business owner still typically maintains his or how complete control over it. There is not a board that typically will vote you out as CEO as the company grows. The main disadvantage is found, in my opinion, in the funding. From a funding standpoint, you are in the same predicament as you are with a sole-proprietorship or partnership. You cannot sell stock to raise funds like with the corporations, but typically, this should not be a deal-breaker for a business owner who is truly determined to succeed.

The last structure that we will discuss is the corporation. I will not go to in-depth on the corporation because of its many complexities, but shall rather focus on a high-level overview. It is definitely recommended that you consult an attorney when setting up your corporation, though many also choose to do it on their own, especially with nonprofit corporations (aka churches). Corporations are truly the most independent businesses in terms of standing on their own as their own entities for tax purposes. They offer the greatest protection from personal liability, and can offer asset protection in regards to the property that the corporation owns for the sake of the business. For instance, your business can own a company vehicle, real estate, and more, and all of the responsibility for any gains or losses in those assets all fall onto the corporation instead of you as an individual. So then, if your traveling is for business, you can consistently drive and fuel the company car from the business's funds instead of your own. Either way, you must still be very smart at how you handle the business finances in addition to your personal finances.

Setting up the corporation is similar to setting up your LLC. You still have to get an EIN/Tax ID just as with all of the other business structures and you will also need to file with the state. When setting up your corporation, you also need to establish board members just as with an LLC. The big difference with a corporation (please note that there are different types, such as the "S" vs the "C" corporation, and each has its own advantages and limitations), you can also register to sell stock, which will be used to raise capital for the business. Many start up corporations will begin selling "penny stocks," or low priced stock options, in order to build the capital necessary to fund the first few years of their business (and often beyond). After you register to sale stocks of your business, you will also then determine the maximum amount that are available for purchase and the amount that you as the owner actually own, because businesses can be purchased right from under the business owner (if not careful) by someone buying up the stock. Also, when you issue stock, you will determine things like how much stock owners will receive in dividends and how often, which is usually tied to company profits. I will leave that part of the discussion there, however, as it just continues to become more complicated as you delve into those topics, and it is best to use a qualified attorney for that area of business.

A final element to consider with the corporation is to make sure that you are extra careful with those who you choose as board members. Remember, the corporation is a stand-alone entity and can be purchased right from under you. Your board members also have the ability to vote you out of the position of CEO, those this type of thing normally doesn't happen until you reach a much higher status and success level. Overall though, the corporation provides the best level of personal liability protection, but also is the most complicated in terms of paperwork and taxes. There are advantages to each structure though, and it is important that you consider all of the benefits and make an informed decision. Choose the structure that works best for what you currently have available, and what will work best with your vision. Then, contact your location government for details on getting a business license, which also has a small fee, plus residual tax payments. Lastly, having well-developed business and marketing plans can also help you determine the best structure, and provide additional guidance along the way.

Business and Marketing Plans

One of the things you will definitely have to learn, or had to learn, if you took standard business classes in college, is how to draft professional business and marketing plans. This plan is something that is also very important for you to create as a part of your foundation. Your business plan is a way for you to really lay out all of the details to your business, including your overall summary of the business, who you are, your products and services, your goals, your market analysis, your financial projections, funds needed, and more. The more thorough this plan is, the better of a guide that it will provide you towards making your business successful. It is not a bad thing, also, to hire a consultant to help you with developing this plan, as you would also present this plan to the bank if you seek them for funding with a business loan.

Your marketing plan is also similar in that it also helps to set the groundwork and guide your progress, but from a marketing perspective. The marketing plan includes market research, details about your target market, competitive analysis, SWOT (strengths, weaknesses, opportunities, threats) analysis, budget details, marketing strategy, and more. The use of these details will help the business owner to make intelligent and informed decisions on how they will advertise and market their products and services in order to yield the most profitable and successful results. This is another key, foundational document for every business owner or entrepreneur to develop in order to have a strong game plan. This is also very important in order to keep focus along the way, and you should consider hiring a consultant to assist with its development as well.

Overall, getting your original paperwork together is vital to establishing the PROPER foundation for your business. This paperwork will help you to keep everything in order as you proceed through your daily, weekly, monthly, etc., activities. A firm foundation is vital in order to properly grow and build, and your paperwork will also protect you from costly mistakes.

CH. 7 – TOUGH BEGINNINGS

Aside from all of the extensive paperwork and foundational details, the start of a new business is an exciting time and a fun adventure. It does have its frustrations, of course, but that comes with anything that you want to do. Even if you are playing a sport, it's not going to be all fun and games because you still have to put in work in the training and practice side of things. In some ways, you could look at entrepreneurship as a type of sport because it is very competitive and requires a lot of consistent, bold, and intense action and commitment by those who participate in it. There are some significant victories that are achieved during the process, and also some losses. In other words, it's not going to be all peaches and cream or rainbows and unicorns. There will be "some good days and some hills to climb," as well as some "weary days, and some lonely nights." But just as that old song says, you must not complain. You must find a way to stay motivated, and to keep the excitement going for yourself. Yet, isn't that one of the key indicators that you are doing the right thing anyway? The work that you do which moves you to be able to push through and motivates you to wake up excited each morning is the very thing that you SHOULD BE doing! Despite that motivation, however, things like a lack of money, a lack of support, and slow growth are hurdles that must be mastered by every would-be entrepreneur. Be ready for them.

Lack of Money

One of the biggest challenges that entrepreneurs face is the lack of capital. Of course, we discussed how some business structures – corporations – give you the option to sell shares to raise capital, but even before you reach that point (as with all structures) you have to find a way to raise the capital that you need on your own. Often, people will start out looking for loans or gifts from family and friends, and the results to this effort can truly vary, depending on the nature of your friends and families. If you do have family members who are capable of providing you with financing, that is great, but very often, the amount of money that they can give you is still limited. That is, these are often one-time gifts and, as such, this money will run out before long. The amount of money needed to run a business must be large enough to cover the long-haul, typically at least seven years of the designated salaries for the owner and workers, as well as enough to cover the expenses of the business for just as long. In fact, when you apply for a business loan, this is the level of financial need that you are seeking, which is also why it can be such a daunting task. Furthermore, banks will typically want for you to have a significant amount of this capital already raised on your own before even considering giving you a loan.

What do we do then? Many entrepreneurs, seeing this challenge, will tap into savings, max out credit cards, liquidate 401k and IRA accounts, or even take out home equity loans or second mortgages in order to fund their businesses if they truly believe in what they are doing. Likewise, there is the old concept of bootstrapping. Essentially, bootstrapping is when you are continually hustling to get your finds. You can do this by continuing to work another full-time job and using a percentage of your earnings to fund your business. You can also regularly run other business efforts like selling products on eBay, or engaging in a paid hobby, then flipping that earned money into personal investments into your primary business efforts. You should typically have about four or more streams of income, so in creating these smaller streams, you can tap into the profits of those to fund the larger stream. Either way, you must use all of the resources that are available in order to keep the financial fuel going, so be creative and don't give up, despite the difficult nature of the process.

Lack of Support

The person who steps out on his or her own quickly learns the meaning of loneliness. You can quote that. One of the major challenges that is faced by an entrepreneur is the limited amount of support that is found in the beginning phases. I emphasize the beginning phases, because once you have gained success and are doing exceedingly well, EVERYBODY is there to support you and talk about how they always believed in you. Getting to that point, however, can be like climbing a huge and difficult mountain. What is even worse about the situation is that the people who you expect to be there the most, family and friends, are often the most disconnected of all. There is a Biblical scripture that teaches that a prophet has no honor in his own town. What this simply means is that those closest to you will have the most difficult time seeing and receiving your greatness. We can understand why though. For all of your life, they've seen you as the little kid from the neighborhood. They watched you grow up, but it's hard to see you beyond all of the growing pains, mistakes, ups and downs, previously failed attempts, and years of excited talk. They don't realize that sometimes it takes years and that so many of the most successful people failed numerous times before finally becoming successful. They don't realize that despite the amount of effort that it takes, you are COMMITTED to making it happen no matter what the cost may be. They also don't realize that you truly have what it takes to succeed. It is very difficult for those closest to you, who have seen your weaknesses and failures, to ever see your potential as they can only see you based on the past.

The other challenge of support from those closest to you is that they "care too much." Your family members and closest friends find it painful to see you struggle to be successful. They'd rather you take the "safe" route and get a job like everyone else because the thought of you losing everything, struggling, losing assets, living in substandard conditions while getting your business off its feet, or going through painful challenges in general, is painful to those who care about you. Then, on top of them feeling sorry for you about the struggles that you may face, they feel obligated to help you stay afloat, which then puts a burden on their shoulders as well, causing them to become vested in the struggle. Yet, those feelings are perfectly normal. This is why, in a lot of cases, family and friends are NOT the ones to turn to when starting something new. You must prepare your mind for this, and understand that it is not as personal as you think. Much of the time, those closest to you are advising you based on their own fears of failure also. This is why your greatest help and support is often found outside of your closest circle and established through networked connections and external investors. Only those who also have an entrepreneurial mentality, and the resources available, can truly understand your struggle. Therefore, don't look at your family and friends' inability to support you as an attack against you, but rather as a weakness that they are unaware of, and thus they are simply incapable of giving you the type of support that you need.

Slow Starts

Another hurdle that makes the beginning stage difficult is found in a lack of patience. Things just are not happening fast enough. I completely understand… You had this vision of money rolling in like a casino jackpot. You saw all of the fame and admiration, and your bank accounts growing exponentially. You imagined new cars, a new house, and rubbing elbows with the city elite. Yet, here you are, "robbing Peter to pay Paul." And, you've been doing this for a while, even with the first six months to a year of bootstrapping and doing freebies for people to build up your experience. This can be a very tough situation to deal with and requires continues self-coaching to be patient and not give up on the dream.

Slow starts can be draining and discouraging. It is important during these times to keep reminding yourself of the vision and telling yourself that YOU WILL GET THERE! Every great journey begins with the first step, but consists of many. Likewise, "the race is not given to the swift or the strong, but to the one who endures until the end," as Biblical scriptures also teach. That endurance is often the one deciding factor of an entrepreneur's success. An important lesson in business, and life in general, is that it takes CONSISTENCY in order to be able to achieve anything significant. How many people fail on their fitness goals because they are not seeing the results they expect fast enough, and so the give up altogether? How many sports teams end up losing a match because they give up in the third quarter instead of continuing to fight hard until the end of the game? How many romantic relationships end after the first argument because they don't want to fight for the relationship to work out? Finally, how many people drop out of high school or college because they didn't have the endurance to finish the years of education? The answer is, way too many. The greater tragedy is that so often, people quit just before reaching their breakthrough. So many times, if they had continued for just a little longer, truly a small fraction of the time that they had already invested, they would've hit the tipping point and been ready for the roller-coaster ride of success. It is very important that you hold on to your vision and keep motivating yourself, even through the slow beginnings. If you don't give up, you will eventually succeed, whether this particular business or an entirely different industry. Ultimately, you cannot give up, despite how tough it gets, if you are to be a successful entrepreneur.

CH. 8 – STAYING MOTIVATED

Remaining motivated is going to be essential to making your business a success. As we discussed in the previous chapter, there are a lot of obstacles and hurdles that will be presented in your path, ranging from financial issues to a lack of support from the people you expect it from the most. These types of challenges are enough to discourage any person in their pursuits, so it is no surprise that any of us would also feel the same way. Nevertheless, because of these challenges, it is that much more imperative that we find an adequate manner to motivate ourselves in whatever business that we are creating.

There are several manners to motivate yourself in pursuit of your entrepreneurial goals. It is important to remember that just like dropping a rock into a pond, the wave is strongest at the center and becomes weaker as it expands outward. So is the same about the energy about your business, or anything else that you do. You are the center of it all, so what you do in terms of enthusiasm and energy is what will pass on to the next person and the next person after that. The more excited that you are, the more contagious that your excitement will be to others, who then continue to pass it on (getting weaker with each level) via word of mouth and other referrals, which we also know is one of the most effective forms of marketing that exists. You must have contagious enthusiasm in your pursuits. The purpose of this chapter, though, is to present methods to have and keep that motivation. Ideally, some key ways to stay motivated are to remember your "why," read motivating material, and network.

Remember Your Why

This is the core of your motivation! On my podcast (www.anchor.fm/kelvinbroadus), I have an entire episode about understanding our "why." This is important because it is truly the reason that we are even pursuing our efforts. That why has to be something powerful enough to get us out of bed each morning and powerful enough to make us face the negativity, challenges, and obstacles that come with any endeavor. That "why" is what causes us to turn the obstacles into opportunities and to fight with all of our might to succeed. It is our passion behind it all, and that passion can be multifaceted.

One element of that passion includes your natural skill and talent; it is something that you feel you were created to do. Passion is often tied to your gifts. Another aspect of your passion is what you are good at doing. There are also the things that move you externally like family and bills. You may know that you have a spouse and kids to take care of and so it is of utmost necessity to keep a reliable source of income that is not capped by corporate limitations. You also are aware of your expenses, such as your mortgage or rent, any vehicle that you own, student loans, or more. Finally, you may simply be fed up with what you have been doing and now greatly need a mental break from it all. Either way, these things that move you to even WANT TO do something new are your reasons why. Therefore, keep yourself in constant remembrance of your why, as this is the motivation to keep pressing on.

Reading Books

If you ask any of the most successful people in

the world what their habits are, I guarantee that reading is one of those habits. And, when I say reading, I am referring to reading BOOKS. By all means, any reading is helpful as it helps to keep the mind sharp and exercise the cognitive functionality of the brain. Reading is truly fundamental. But, it is also very important to read for personal growth and motivation.

I will always remember a lesson that I learned from a mentor at a company that I used to work at telling me that one of the books that he learned from to help him reach his personal level of success was the "Art of War." I was able to literally watch him apply the principles in business to his role, and watched him climb the corporate ladder with amazing skill and power to the highest level so executive leadership. If you follow any of the major thought leaders, CEOs, and other top ranking business leaders, you will hear them discuss the habit of reading daily, book after book. You will do well to read books that are related to your specific industry in order to continually grow in ideas and skills. Please note, however, that industry related magazines, blogs, etc., are also very beneficial. Reading books related to personal motivation and growth, as well as general business topics such as time and money management and selling, is also very important along the way. We are all busy, and watching movies and television are definitely easier to do, but taking the time to sacrifice entertainment for mental development via reading will pay off tremendously over time. The committed business owner must understand that playtime (entertainment) is more of a reward for hard work and responsibility, and will prioritize personal growth over personal entertainment. That way, when you do succeed, you will have far greater results and be able to celebrate even greater than if you did it prematurely.

Networking

In addition to remembering your "why" and actively reading motivational books, we must also look at the value of networking. Networking is the practice of meeting and exchanging value with other people. Think about it, there's an old saying that no man is an island unto himself. In other words, we cannot do it (life) alone, and if we do, it will be much more difficult that if we had support and interaction with others. Even when you look at the basic premise of any business, nothing happens until a sale is made, but a sale requires someone else making a purchase. We, as people, need each other, especially in business and entrepreneurship.

When we consider networking, there are typically two recommended forms to consider, and those are industry events and personal networking. Depending on the industry that you are in, there are often a variety of professional organizations related to that industry. Marketers have marketing organizations, salespeople have sales organizations, and so forth. These organizations have many different functions from simply fellowship to offering specialized certifications and educational opportunities to their members. They also have a cost, so if you consider joining one (which is often a good idea because of the opportunities that become available to you through these organizations) then just keep that in mind. Beyond industry specific, professional organizations, there are also events that are not specific to any industry, but that rather cover a variety of topics and industries. Many of the top thought leaders, such as Tony Robbins or Brendon Burchard, will host regular motivational seminars that can be attended by anyone. Though these events can sometimes be costly, there are often a variety of discounts offered to people on their mailing lists, and the relationships developed in these sessions can be very valuable. Sometimes it is for the best to invest in yourself for these types of events because the value that you gain from the knowledge shared and new points of contact can easily outweigh the cost of the investment, giving you a large return on your investment. Likewise, in addition to all of the educational value that you gain, the motivation factor is very strong at these events. Attendees are typically very excited and pumped up during, and after the completion of, these events, which they later carry over into their businesses.

Personal Networking

The third of these recommendations is to network with others on a personal level. Personal networking is as essential as the traditional effort of passing out business cards. In fact, keeping business cards is still a viable method of establishing your personal network. You network on a personal level when you attend the aforementioned events, but also anywhere that you go. I have had people come up to me and talk about their businesses in the grocery store or at the mall. Many times, you can find a young musical artist at the mall standing around handing out or trying to sell their CDs to shoppers that are passing by them. I remember one very dedicated musician who sold me a copy of his CD at the gas station when I was going to the store. As a result, I ended up actually promoting him a little more via word-of-mouth, which is a desired.

In general, your personal network is going to be a portion of your clientele or customer base, but as we discussed earlier, sometimes it takes those closest to you a little longer to warm up to the idea of you being a businessperson. But, that personal network will be a good source of motivation and word-of-mouth support for you to help push the vision further than you can do by yourself. The most vital people that you network with are those who also are excited about what you are doing and who are passionate about your "cause" or company mission. These supporters might even be willing to invest in your company, or at least be the ones who helped you out with loans in the initial stages of raising capital. Also, remember that networking doesn't have to be that difficult. The most challenging part will be you striking up a conversation with strangers, but eventually this will become fun as it allows you to talk about the things that you are passionate about, primarily, your new business. Overall though, the better that you network is, the more that it will motivate you to keep going, if not for you then for them. It is a little more difficult to give up when you see how what you are doing positively impacts those who are around you.

Positive Self-Talk (Bonus)

Last but not least, let's consider a final point of motivation, which is continuous positive self-talk. Another habit of the successful is to use daily positive affirmations. You might typically develop a list of about ten affirmations that align with your financial, health, spiritual, and mental goals (you can develop more of them if you need). Then, at the start of each day, speak these affirmations over yourself over and over, even up to 100 times. If you are driving to a location for work, especially if your entrepreneurial ventures are in addition to a full-time job, then you can go as far as recording your affirmations and playing them on the radio for the entire time of your drive. Likewise, for every negative thought, challenge it with three positive thoughts to replace it.

Understand, it is easy to be discouraged on any given day because of the things on the news, the detractors in the industry, and naysayers. Because of the very nature of the human psyche, the mind will automatically calculate the negative possibilities in any situation, so it doesn't take much for you to spend each day going over negative ideas about your dreams. Sadly, far too many people are their worst enemies in terms of self-talk, and speak more harshly about themselves than the people around them ever would. This is why it is so important that as an entrepreneur, you surround yourself with positivity. You should attend positive and motivating seminars, join positive organizations, network with positive people, and speak positivity to yourself each and every day. Keep all of these things that we've talked about in mind, and before you know it, you will be running a new, successful business. It doesn't stop there though, as well see in the next and final chapter.

CH. 9 – DIVERSIFYING OPTIONS

When we look at all of the time, commitment, and effort that it takes to build a successful business, to actually start something and do so something of your own, it can be quite impressive and overwhelming. Think about all of the effort, from simply putting in the work to overcome your fears after retraining your mind to believe that you even DESERVED better than what you were getting, to patiently working through all of the intricate details to make it happen. It is more than just a fluke of an idea, and more than just a hobby. When you decide to step out on your own and take that leap of faith to start something new, you are releasing a part of yourself into the business that you are creating. It is a part of you, which is why so many entrepreneurs will refer to their business as their baby.

Just like with a baby, you plan it; well, sometimes you didn't plan it at all but you became so overwhelmed in your passion (talking about the business here) that it just had to come forth. You went through all of the checks and balances to ensure that the business would be healthy just as a pregnant woman goes through all of the health procedures like taking vitamins and attending doctor visits. A business also can take many months to properly plan and prepare for unveiling. Then once the business goes live (is birthed), you are extra careful to do everything right, staying up late nights and addressing every issue that pops up to make sure that it gets off to a great start. You nurture that business and over time it eventually reaches a place where it can stand on its own and you can relax more as it is in an auto-pilot type of stage, similar to children reaching their teen years. This is where the concept of diversifying your options comes in.

In the previous centuries, large families were seen as a thing of greatness. Families sought to have as many kids as possible, as it was a sign of wealth and helped to assure the strength of the family. Though society has largely moved past this ideal, it still represents a strong business concept. That is, the more businesses – streams of income – that you have, the more financially stable that you become. Ideally, you would do well with at least four stable streams of income, and surely not relying on your job alone. After all, companies do layoffs, go through acquisitions, and close down every day. Because of this, it is very wise to start and do your own thing, even if just for the sake of having these extra streams of income. Don't get me wrong, it is possible to be fully successful and have an enjoyable life with just one stream or just one business, but a well-known "secret" of successful business leaders is that you start businesses with the eventual goal of selling them and living off of the profits. At the least, you pass on the leadership of the business to others while remaining on the board. Even when you look at the analogy of kids, they will eventually grow up and move on to become independent and primarily "belong" to their own, new families. Just the same is a profitable direction for your entrepreneurial ventures.

When your business becomes stable enough to stand on its own, consider starting a new business. This way, you not only will be establishing new income for yourself, but you will also be enhancing your business skill sets and growing your credibility. By diversifying your business portfolio, you will keep things more exciting and help break up the monotony that can be found in doing the same thing over and over again. You will even find that most entrepreneurs become "serial entrepreneurs" because of them understanding this concept. You don't even have to sell the businesses that you start, but can have a large portfolio of businesses that run themselves, providing you with a lot of passive income for your general oversight of many things. Either way, diversify.

A great example that I've seen for diversifying options is a friend who has multiple businesses. I first was aware of her daycare business. It started with one 24-hour location, and eventually expanded with her opening another location in a different city. Then, I noticed that she had a bookkeeping business, while still owning the daycare. Now she has added a CPR training business that is across different states. All of these businesses operate independently of each other, but all are practical and valuable services. Likewise, who knows what other smaller ventures she maintains that are not as public. This is a perfect illustration of what it means to diversify your options.

Another guy that I know also really takes this concept seriously. He started out being involved in an MLM company as an Independent Business Owner (IBO). After gaining pretty good success in that, recruiting other people and expanding his network, he eventually stepped out and developed his own platform doing the same sort of thing. Since then he has started a drop-shipping business using one of the major online platforms (and teaches others how to do the same), he runs a digital marketing agency and also teaches others to develop their own, and he is even venturing into the CBD oil industry. The great thing about this entrepreneur is that he does practically every business online. Yes, he has his own physical location, but all of the services that he develops can be seen as online businesses, and they all have a type of affiliate process, or training to teach others how to do the same. I guess that you could say that his entrepreneurial training is a business of its own, and his marketing of all of it is phenomenal.

One final example that I'd like to share is for a friend who does great social media marketing for his financial business brand. It is very clever and catchy, and also provides an example of another type of diversification. Sometimes you don't have to diversify based on different businesses, but can diversify WITHIN the same business by offering different services that are based on different divisions within. Under this entrepreneur's overall brand, there are multiple different types of product offerings, all connected but still different. Within his financial company, his product suite includes insurance products, investment products, credit repair services, publishing, helping other businesses obtain capital to get started, and even has an academy attached to teach others and the youth about general financial and business principles. And, because of his emphasis on branding, he is able to also branded products, from t-shirts to stationary to books, that all continue to promote his business further.

In all of these examples, we continue to find the same concept though. That concept is continual growth. It is important to never become stagnant, but continue to advance yourself. As I write this book, I am reminded of the mentality that I have also possessed, and entrepreneurship has always (and probably WILL ALWAYS be) been a part of my goals. I've had some successes and some failures, but I continue to start and do because that is the only way prevent being trapped by circumstances out of your control. I believe, as someone wise once said a long time ago, that you should have multiple streams of income. In such, I encourage you to also – at the least – try to start something and do something new for yourself. Everyone might not be successful as a big time entrepreneur, but starting something extra is definitely helpful. Believe in yourself and keep making moves. On that note, I'll end with a scripture from the Biblical book of Ecclesiastes, chapter 11 and verse 6. It says:

"In the morning sow thy seed, and in the evening

withhold not thin hand: for thou knowest not whether shall prosper, either this or that, or whether they both shall be alike good."

ABOUT THE AUTHOR

Kelvin N. Broadus is the author of "Start Something, Do Something," as well as other books such as his original book of poetry, "Creative Expressions." His professional experience includes nearly two decades in the corporate training and communications fields. As an entrepreneur, he has ventured into media publishing, motivational speaking and life/business coaching, music and video production, and also the fitness industry. He also has a foundation in nonprofit and ministry work.

www.ingramcontent.com/pod-product-compliance
Lightning Source LLC
Chambersburg PA
CBHW031433210526
45464CB00005B/2175